D1490547

BROOKLYN
NETS

by Ray Frager

249 2906

b /20745380

796.323
F

Published by ABDO Publishing Company, 8000 West 78th Street, Edina, Minnesota 55439. Copyright © 2012 by Abdo Consulting Group, Inc. International copyrights reserved in all countries. No part of this book may be reproduced in any form without written permission from the publisher. SportsZone™ is a trademark and logo of ABDO Publishing Company.

Printed in the United States of America,
North Mankato, Minnesota
062011
082013
Revised Edition 2014

 THIS BOOK CONTAINS AT LEAST 10% RECYCLED MATERIALS.

Editors: Matt Tustison, Dave McMahon
Copy Editor: Nicholas Cafarelli
Series design: Christa Schneider
Cover production: Craig Hinton
Interior production: Carol Castro

Photo Credits: Kathy Willens/AP Images, cover, 38; Julio Cortez/AP Images, 1; AP Images, 4, 15, 16, 23, 24, 27, 42 (top); Lennox McLendon/AP Images, 7; Richard Drew/AP Images, 8, 42 (bottom); Jim Cummins/NBAE/Getty Images, 10; NBAE/Getty Images, 12; John Rooney/AP Images, 18; Focus on Sport/Getty Images, 20, 42 (middle); Marty Lederhandler/AP Images, 29; Andy Hayt/Getty Images, 30; Ron Frehm/AP Images, 33; Tim DeFrisco/Getty Images, 34, 43 (top); Bill Kostroun/AP Images, 36, 43 (middle); Mary Altaffer/AP Images, 42, 43 (bottom); Morry Gash/AP Images, 44; Sipa via AP Images, 47

Library of Congress Cataloging-in-Publication Data
Frager, Ray.
  Brooklyn Nets / by Ray Frager.
     p. cm. -- (Inside the NBA)
  Includes index.
  ISBN 978-1-61783-166-9
  1. New Jersey Nets (Basketball team)--History--Juvenile literature. I. Title.
  GV885.52.N37F73 2012
  796.323'640974932--dc22
                       2011014418

TABLE OF CONTENTS

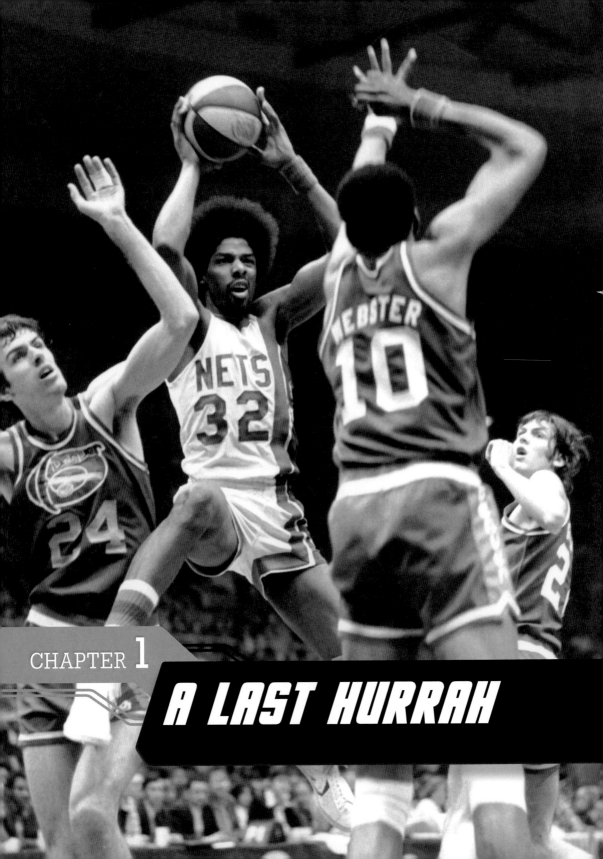

CHAPTER 1

A LAST HURRAH

Before the Brooklyn Nets entered the National Basketball Association (NBA), they were members of a rival league, the American Basketball Association (ABA). In fact, the Nets hold an important place in ABA history. They played in the ABA's last game and were the league's last champions.

That championship came in 1976 when the Nets, then called the New York Nets, defeated the Denver Nuggets four games to two in the ABA Finals. The Nets were led by probably the greatest player in ABA history and one of the most exciting pro basketball players ever, Julius "Dr. J" Erving.

The ABA existed from 1967 to 1976. In that last 1975–76 season of the ABA, Erving was the league's leading scorer. He averaged 29.3 points per game. The 6-foot-6 forward was helped

The Nets' Julius Erving, "Dr. J," goes up with the ball against the Denver Nuggets in February 1976. Erving led his team to a title that year in the ABA's final season.

JULIUS ERVING

In playing for the Nets from 1973 to 1976, Julius Erving was coming home. Erving grew up in Roosevelt, New York, not far from where the Nets played in Uniondale.

Erving played five seasons in the ABA. The former University of Massachusetts standout spent his first two professional seasons with the ABA's Virginia Squires before he joined the Nets. Erving won three scoring titles and three Most Valuable Player (MVP) Awards in the ABA. After the ABA and the NBA merged, he played for 11 seasons in the NBA, though with the Philadelphia 76ers, not the Nets.

He apparently received the "Doctor" nickname in high school from a friend who was responding to how Erving always called him "Professor." However, as Erving's basketball legend grew, fans came to appreciate how the high-flying Dr. J "operated" on the basketball court.

out by the Nets' backcourt of Brian Taylor and "Super" John Williamson. The two combined to average nearly 33 points per game.

The Nets played their home games at Nassau Veterans Memorial Coliseum in Uniondale, New York. That town is on Long Island, just outside New York City. The Nets had challenged the Knicks of the NBA for popularity among New York fans. This was because of the wide-open style in the ABA and the acrobatic play of Erving.

In the 1975–76 season, the Nets went 55–29. They finished five games behind the league's best record by the Denver Nuggets. In the ABA semifinals, the Nets faced the San Antonio Spurs. The Spurs lost their top scorer, James Silas, to an injury in the first game of the series. But they

The Nets' Brian Taylor, *left*, defends the Spurs' George Gervin during Game 7 of the 1976 ABA semifinals. The Nets prevailed 121–114.

took the Nets to the full seven games of the series. The Spurs featured a player who was just as creative as Erving, George Gervin. Gervin averaged 27.1 points against the Nets in the series. Still, playing before a sellout crowd at home, the Nets won Game 7 by seven points to

Familiar Faces

When the Nets played the Spurs in the 1976 ABA semifinals, they were facing two former teammates. Larry Kenon and Billy Paultz had played for the Nets before being traded to the Spurs. Each had a distinctive nickname. Kenon, who shared some of Julius Erving's athletic moves, was called "Dr. K." Paultz, a wide-bodied center, was called "The Whopper."

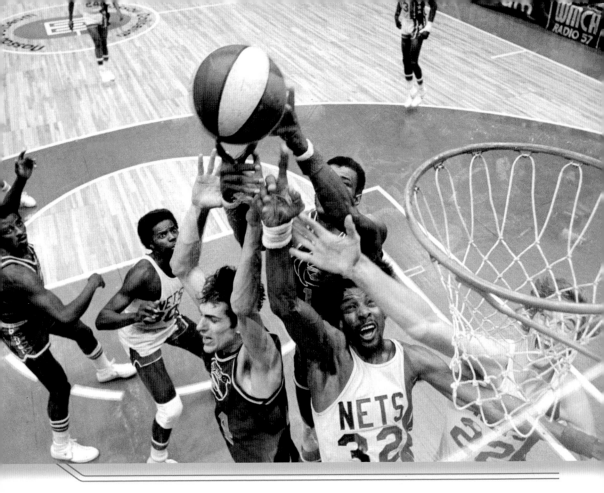

New York's Julius Erving (32) and Jim Eakins (22) go after the ball against Denver in Game 6 of the 1976 ABA Finals. The Nets won 112–106 for their second ABA title.

Master Inventor

"A young Julius Erving was like Thomas Edison; he was always inventing something new every night."
—Former pro basketball player, coach, and broadcaster Johnny Kerr

reach the ABA Finals against the Nuggets.

The Nuggets had produced a 60–24 regular-season record with a powerful lineup. Their leading scorer, forward David Thompson, was an impressive leaper. He was nicknamed

"Skywalker." He would soar over other players on his way to averaging 26 points. Denver also had Dan Issel, a center who scored 23 points per game, and equally high-scoring guard Ralph Simpson.

Game 1 of the Finals was played at McNichols Sports Arena in Denver. The crowd of 19,034 set a record for attendance at an ABA game. Erving made a shot at the buzzer—part of his 45 points—to win the game for the Nets. The Nuggets came back to win Game 2. Then the Nets won the next two games at Nassau Coliseum. The Nuggets won Game 5 back in Denver.

In Game 6 on Long Island, it looked as if the Nuggets were going to force a seventh game. They took a 22-point lead in the third quarter. But the Nets were determined to end the series and win the championship in front of their home fans. They staged a big rally in the fourth quarter. They turned up their defense, pressing the Nuggets in the backcourt. Key baskets by Williamson and Jim Eakins allowed the Nets to catch up to and pass the Nuggets for a 112–106 victory and the ABA championship.

It was the last game played in the league. And through the 2012–13 season, it was the last time the Nets had won any league title.

Nets Pay to Play

After the NBA and the ABA merged in 1976, four ABA teams were allowed to enter the NBA—the Nets, the San Antonio Spurs, the Denver Nuggets, and the Indiana Pacers. The Nets had to pay $8 million for the right to join the NBA. Of that amount, $3.2 million went to the NBA, and $4.8 million was for the New York Knicks because the Nets would be operating a team in the Knicks' "territory."

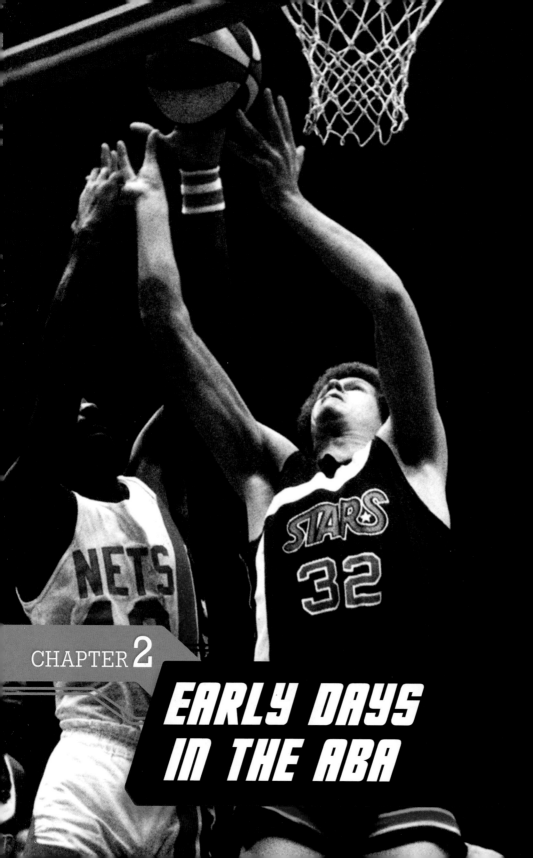

CHAPTER 2

EARLY DAYS
IN THE ABA

The Brooklyn Nets began life as the New Jersey Americans. The team was a charter member of the ABA. The league played its inaugural season in 1967–68 with 11 clubs.

The ABA originally wanted a team in New York City because that was and still is the biggest center for media attention in the United States. The ABA hoped that with a team in New York, the whole country would take notice of the new league. However, the Americans could not find an arena in Manhattan in which to play. So they ended up outside New York, in nearby Teaneck, New Jersey. They played in an armory converted into a basketball arena.

Living One Day at a Time

"*[The ABA] always seemed one step ahead of extinction, franchises seeming to move or fold on an almost daily basis.*"
—Billy Reed, sports columnist

Nets center Willie Sojourner, *left*, battles near the basket against the Utah Stars during the 1974–75 ABA season.

Team owner Arthur Brown knew it was not an ideal way to start a new franchise. But it was not exactly an ideal team either. Most of the roster had little professional experience and did not last long as pro players. The first coach was Max Zaslofsky. He had been an NBA star in the 1940s and 1950s.

The Americans' first star was Levern "Jelly" Tart. He joined the club halfway through the first season after starting out with the Oakland Oaks. Tart, a 6-foot-2 guard, averaged 19 points for the Americans in 1967–68.

The Americans went through 17 players that first season. Only seven of them

Nets center Dan Anderson poses in the late 1960s. An original member of the franchise, Anderson averaged 14.7 points and 11 rebounds in the 1967–68 season.

FLOOR FORFEIT

The New Jersey Americans and the Kentucky Colonels finished the ABA's first season with 36–42 records. That tied them for fourth place—and the last playoff spot—in the Eastern Division. To decide which team would reach the Eastern semifinal series, a one-game playoff was scheduled.

The Americans could not hold the game on their home court at the Teaneck Armory in New Jersey. The armory was occupied by a circus. Instead, the Americans found a temporary home at the Commack Arena on Long Island. The basketball court was not ready, however. The floor had not been installed correctly, with parts of it loose.

The commissioner of the ABA, George Mikan, decided that the Americans, as the home team, would have to forfeit the game to Kentucky. The Colonels went on to participate in the playoffs without actually having to face the Americans.

played any games for the team the next season. The club's average home attendance was fewer than 1,000 fans. The Americans had a 36–42 record in 1967–68 and tied for the last playoff spot in the Eastern Division. What was their strength? Shooting free throws. The Americans ranked second in the ABA in foul shooting.

In a bizarre ending to the season, the Americans had to forfeit their one-game playoff against the Kentucky Colonels. This was because the condition of their temporary home court in Commack, New York, was unsuitable for play.

Even though the Americans' first season ended with forfeiting the one-game playoff at the Commack Arena, that is exactly where the team moved for the 1968–69 season.

Brown wanted to get "New York" in his team's name to help attract more attention from the big city. To go along with the change in first name, he also changed the rest of the name. So the New Jersey Americans became the New York Nets.

The Nets went on to a dismal season, going 17–61. It was the worst record in the ABA. After the season, Brown sold the team to businessman Roy Boe.

The ABA was competing with the NBA for the best basketball players. The top player coming out of college in 1969 was center Lew Alcindor from the University of California, Los Angeles (UCLA). Alcindor grew up in New York. The ABA gave the Nets the rights to try signing him. They hoped he would want to play near his hometown rather than with the NBA's Milwaukee Bucks, who had drafted him. Nevertheless, Alcindor chose Milwaukee.

Star center Lew Alcindor, shown in 1969 while he was at UCLA, decided to sign with the NBA's Milwaukee Bucks after college rather than his hometown New York Nets.

Alcindor later changed his name to Kareem Abdul-Jabbar and scored more than 38,000 points, an NBA record, during his long career.

For 1969–70, the Nets would play in West Hempstead, New York. This was still on Long Island but closer to New York City. Attendance was three times higher than the season before. Things were better on the court, too. Tart, the team's leading scorer in its first season, returned after being traded. He was again the Nets' top scorer at 24.2 points per game. His partner at guard was

Bill Melchionni. Melchionni jumped to the ABA from the NBA's Philadelphia 76ers and averaged 15.2 points. The Nets went 39–45 and made the playoffs for the first time. However, they lost their series to the Kentucky Colonels four games to three.

Things got even more exciting for the 1970–71 season. Lou Carnesecca, a popular college coach at St. John's University in New York, took over as coach. More importantly, the Nets picked up Rick Barry. He was one of pro basketball's outstanding players. Barry, a high-scoring forward, had left the NBA's San Francisco Warriors for the ABA's Oakland Oaks in 1968. He stayed with the club when it moved to Washington DC

Impossible to Guard?

Bill Sharman, Rick Barry's coach with the NBA's San Francisco Warriors, had high praise for Barry's abilities on offense: "He has to be the quickest [6-foot-7] player the game of basketball has ever seen. He's awfully hard, if not impossible, to match up against defensively. He beats a bigger opponent with his quickness and goes over the little man. He is unstoppable going to the basket on a one-on-one situation and is usually successful one-on-two. . . . He has all the shots—the hook, jumper, fadeaway, set, and the layups with either or both hands."

in 1969. But when it moved to Virginia in 1970, Barry did not want to go. Instead, he went to the Nets.

Barry put in two terrific seasons with the Nets. He ended second in the ABA in scoring two years in a row. He averaged 29.4 points in 1970–71 and 31.5 in 1971–72. Barry had

The Nets' Rick Barry (24) blocks a shot attempt by the Squires' Doug Moe in January 1972. Barry helped the Nets reach their first ABA Finals that year.

Nets owner Roy Boe, *right*, poses with Nassau County executive Ralph Caso in 1972 inside Nassau Veterans Memorial Coliseum, the team's then-new arena.

many outstanding qualities as a basketball player. He was a heads-up passer who found open teammates in addition to being a great scorer. He also had a distinctive way of shooting free throws. Barry shot them underhanded, an old-fashioned way that practically no one else still used. But Barry was deadly on free throws. He made about nine out of 10 and almost always ranked among the best in whatever league he played.

The Nets finished 40–44 in Barry and Carnesecca's first season. This was good for third place in the Eastern Division and a spot in the playoffs. They lost, however, in the first round to the Virginia Squires.

In 1971–72, the Nets were even better. They had their first winning season at 44–40. Their first-round playoff opponent was the Kentucky Colonels. The Colonels had set an ABA record with 68 wins. But the Nets opened the series with two victories on the Colonels' home court and won the matchup four games to two.

In the next round, the Nets got past the Squires in seven games to reach the ABA Finals for the first time. Against the Indiana Pacers, the Nets played a close series. But Indiana took the title four games to two.

During that season, the Nets moved once again. This time it was to Nassau Veterans Memorial Coliseum in Uniondale, New York. The attendance at Nassau Coliseum averaged 12,000 fans. This was a long way from the 1,000 who used to come out for games in Teaneck.

However, before the 1972–73 season, Barry was forced to return to the NBA because of a judge's ruling. Without Barry, the Nets fell to 30–54 and a first-round loss in the playoffs.

Before the 1973–74 season, though, the Nets made one of the most important trades in their history. They acquired an even bigger star than Barry, Julius Erving, from the Squires.

You Have to Go Back

Rick Barry was enjoying the spotlight of playing in New York, and the Nets were becoming more successful since he joined the team. But in the late 1960s and early 1970s, players were jumping back and forth between the NBA and the ABA. In Barry's case, his former NBA team, the San Francisco Warriors, had gone to court to try getting Barry back from the ABA. A judge ruled he had to return to the NBA team. After two seasons with the Nets, Barry went back to San Francisco.

CHAPTER 3

GLORY WITH THE DOC

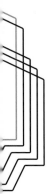

W hen Julius Erving joined the New York Nets for the 1973–74 season, he helped form a young but extremely talented lineup.

None of the five starters was older than 25. Two were rookies, forward Larry Kenon and guard John Williamson. They combined with guard Brian Taylor, center Billy Paultz, and forward Erving.

Erving led the league in scoring at 27.4 points per game.

He also averaged 5.2 assists on his way to being named the ABA's MVP. Erving, Kenon, and Paultz each averaged more than 10 rebounds per game. The Nets finished first in the Eastern Division with a 55–29 record. In the playoffs, they lost only two games while winning

Julius Erving rises for one of his trademark slams in the 1970s. The Nets won the ABA title in 1974 in Erving's first season with the team.

three series. The Nets finished the season by defeating the Utah Stars four games to one for their first league championship.

Along the way, Erving raised the profile of the Nets in New York and across the country. He was featured on the cover of *Sports Illustrated* for the first time in January 1974. The photograph showed him around the rim with a headline of "What's up? Doc J." Before the next season, the Nets even added one of the longtime stars from the New York Knicks, Dave DeBusschere, as general manager.

Erving's exciting arrival with the Nets was described in the *New York Post*: "The Knicks don't have the only pro basketball team in town. The Nets are now in business, too. They've got to be reckoned with. They'll get their crowd as well, and Dr. J. will deserve the credit. He's the only man, as they say, who has a Ph.D. in basketball."

During the 1974–75 season, Erving again excelled. He led the Nets in scoring, rebounding, and assists. The team was essentially unchanged from the previous championship season. But the Nets fell in the first round of the playoffs to the Spirits of St. Louis. The Spirits had a losing record in

Whopper of a Player

Billy Paultz, the center on the Nets' first championship team, was 6 feet 11 inches tall but did not look like a basketball player. He weighed about 250 pounds and had a chubby physique. But Paultz was a good outside shooter for a center, which could cause problems for other teams. And he knew how to be an effective rebounder. He quickly became popular with Nets fans, some of whom would hang a banner in Nassau Coliseum that read: "Welcome to Paultz's Palace." He was called "The Whopper" because of his weight and because he liked to eat hamburgers.

Julius Erving poses before a game in April 1974. With the Nets, "Dr. J" was named MVP of the ABA in 1974 and 1976 and co-MVP in 1975.

the regular season. The Nets reacted to their loss by trading two of their starters, Kenon and Paultz.

It worked out very well, though. The Nets, with Erving leading the way, won the final ABA championship in 1976.

A Controversial Move

The Knicks were not happy that one of their stars, Dave DeBusschere, joined the Nets as general manager after he retired as a player. The Nets, as part of the rival ABA, were challenging the Knicks for fans in New York. DeBusschere helped lead the Knicks to two championships. But the team waited seven years after he had finished playing to honor him by retiring his number. Some basketball followers thought the Knicks took that long to get over being mad at DeBusschere.

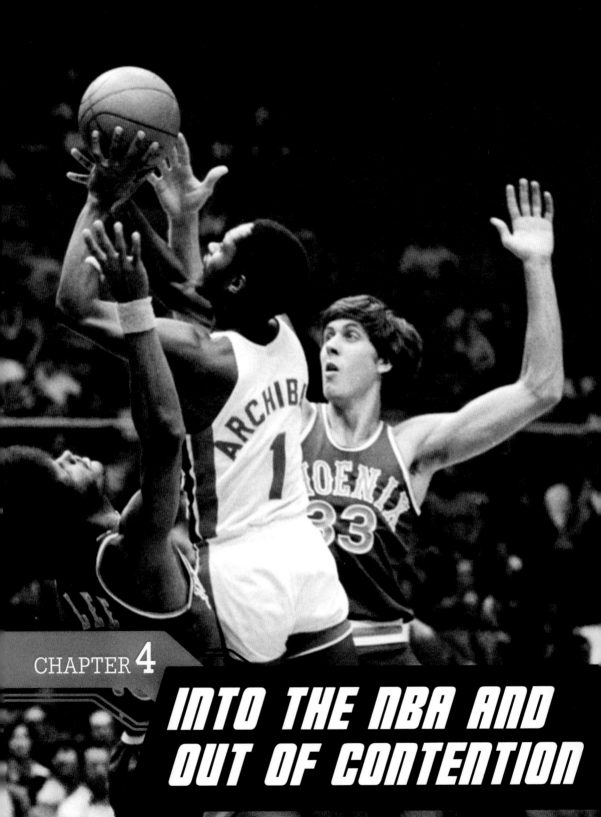

CHAPTER 4

INTO THE NBA AND OUT OF CONTENTION

T he ABA shut down because of financial struggles in 1976. Along with the Denver Nuggets, the Indiana Pacers, and the San Antonio Spurs, the Nets joined the NBA for the 1976–77 season.

Unfortunately for the Nets, they began play in the NBA without Julius Erving. Dr. J was seeking a new, larger contract from the Nets. Roy Boe, the team's owner, did not want to give him one. Boe was concerned that all of Erving's magnificent leaping would soon take a toll on his knees. The owner did not want to end up paying a lot of money to a player who would be injured most of the time. Erving had led the Nets to two ABA championships. He did not like being

Nate "Tiny" Archibald shoots against the Suns in December 1976. Archibald was injured for most of his first season with the Nets, who went 22–60 in their inaugural NBA campaign.

Tiny Hopes

The Nets probably expected a lot when they traded for Nate "Tiny" Archibald before their first season in the NBA. Archibald, a clever, lightning-quick guard, had made NBA history in 1972–73 while with the Kansas City-Omaha Kings. Archibald averaged 34 points and 11.4 assists, becoming the first player in NBA history to lead the league in scoring and assists in the same season. However, Archibald played only 34 games for the Nets before he was injured. After the 1976–77 season, the club traded him to the Buffalo Braves.

paid less than Nate Archibald, a top NBA guard the team had obtained.

The disagreement dragged on as the Nets began to practice for the new season without Erving. Boe also needed money to pay fees for entry into the NBA. So he traded Dr. J to the Philadelphia 76ers for $3 million.

"I had an inclination we'd lose him," said Kevin Loughery, who was then coach of the Nets. "Roy was a good owner, one of the best I'd worked for. . . . He wanted to win. But the situation was one of finances."

Without Erving and also without Archibald for much of the season after he was injured, the Nets posted the NBA's worst record in 1976–77 at 22–60. The Nets were a far different team from the one that won the ABA title. Not only was Erving gone, but guards Brian Taylor and "Super" John Williamson also were traded. Only five of the championship Nets were still with the team by the end of that first NBA season.

The Nets moved back to New Jersey in their second NBA season. They made their home at the Rutgers Athletic Center at Rutgers University in Piscataway. This took the team farther away from the spotlight of New York City. The Nets'

Robert "Bubbles" Hawkins leaves the court after he scored 44 points to help the Nets beat the Jazz 93–89 in overtime in February 1977.

new home was 40 miles (64 km) from "the Big Apple."

The Nets finished with the NBA's worst record again in 1977–78, though they won four more games. That season, the team became known as the New Jersey Nets rather than the New York Nets. In 1978–79, the Nets improved enough to at least make the playoffs. They still had a losing record

Bubbling Up

During the Nets' first NBA season, one of their top players was guard Robert "Bubbles" Hawkins. The Golden State Warriors released Hawkins before the 1976–77 season. He was about to take a job outside of basketball when the Nets called during the season. Hawkins averaged about 20 points in 52 games. However, he played in just 19 games over the next two seasons, the final one with the Detroit Pistons. His career was over after the 1978–79 campaign.

at 37–45, however. The Nets quickly exited the playoffs in the first round. The next two seasons produced losing records again. The Nets did not qualify for the postseason either time.

In 1977, the Nets drafted Bernard King. He was a promising forward from the University of Tennessee. But before King could develop into a star, they traded him. In 1979, another rookie forward, Calvin Natt, was enjoying a productive first season. He was averaging nearly 20 points. But the team traded him. The Nets suddenly were an older team.

Before the 1978–79 season, Boe got out of the NBA. He sold the Nets to a group led by Joseph Taub and Alan Cohen.

By 1980–81, the Nets started to add younger talent.

With the sixth and seventh selections in the draft, they picked forward Mike O'Koren from the University of North Carolina and center Mike Gminski from Duke University. As the team prepared to move into a new arena, the Nets also changed coaches. Loughery was fired. Larry Brown was hired to take over the next season. Brown had been a successful coach in the ABA.

Forward Mike O'Koren, *right*, and center Mike Gminski shake hands after the Nets chose them sixth and seventh overall in the 1980 NBA Draft.

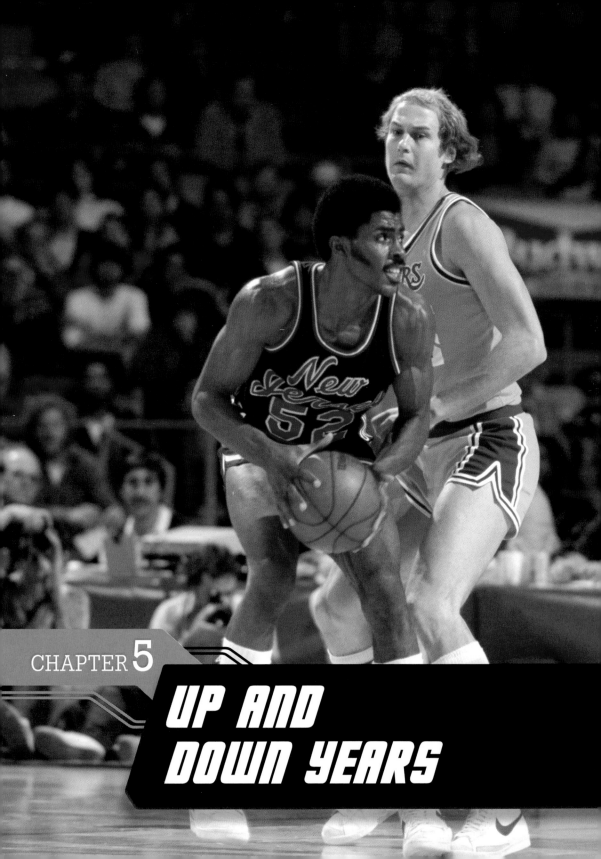

CHAPTER 5

UP AND DOWN YEARS

T he 1981–82 season brought a lot of change to the Nets. First, they moved into the new Brendan Byrne Arena in East Rutherford, New Jersey. The Nets averaged just fewer than 14,000 fans per game. This was fourth best in the NBA.

Things were different on the court, too. Larry Brown had taken over as coach, and the roster underwent changes. The Nets had drafted power forward Buck Williams. He averaged 15.5 points and 12.3 rebounds on his way to being named NBA Rookie of the Year. The Nets also acquired a new set of

What's Your Name?

When the Nets began playing in their new arena in East Rutherford, New Jersey, the site was called Brendan Byrne Arena. It was named after a former governor of New Jersey. It kept that name until 1996, when a sponsor bought the rights to call it the Continental Airlines Arena. The arena was also named the Izod Center. The Nets moved to the Prudential Center in Newark, New Jersey, in 2010.

Nets forward Buck Williams posts up the Lakers' Mark Landsberger in the early 1980s. Williams, a standout rebounder, played for the Nets from 1981 to 1989.

DAWKINS THE DUNKER

Darryl Dawkins entered the NBA with the Philadelphia 76ers in 1975, becoming the first player to be drafted right out of high school. Philadelphia selected Dawkins, a Florida native, with the fifth overall pick in the 1975 NBA Draft.

Dawkins had many productive seasons with the 76ers before the team traded him to the Nets before the 1982–83 campaign for a first-round draft pick. Dawkins continued to be a reliable scorer and rebounder while with the Nets. The muscular, 6-foot-10 Dawkins was even more famous, however, for shattering glass backboards with his strong dunks. He would give his dunks names, such as "In-Your-Face Disgrace" and "Look Out Below."

Dawkins's dunks helped lead to changes. Backboards are now made of shatterproof material, and rims are designed with springs so they can bend instead of break.

guards, Ray Williams and Otis Birdsong. Ray Williams led the team in scoring at 20.4 points a contest.

The Nets improved their record by 20 games over the previous season. They finished 44–38. They made the playoffs as a result. However, they were eliminated in the first round.

The better season did not mean the Nets kept the same team together, though, for 1982–83. Ray Williams was traded for another guard, Phil Ford. Ford then soon was traded for forward Mickey Johnson. Johnson became part of still another trade. This one brought guard Micheal Ray Richardson to New Jersey. The Nets also added center Darryl Dawkins. Despite so many changes, the Nets went 49–33 and qualified for the playoffs again.

Darryl Dawkins tries to block a shot by the Bucks' Jack Sikma in 1986. Dawkins was a force around the basket for the Nets for several seasons.

The Nets did not finish the season with Brown as their coach, however. He took the job as coach at the University of Kansas. The Nets finished up under interim coach Bill Blair. They then were eliminated again in the first round of the postseason.

In 1983–84, the Nets made it past the first round of the playoffs. They defeated the defending NBA champions, the Philadelphia 76ers, before

The Nets' Drazen Petrovic takes a jump shot in January 1991. Petrovic died in a car accident after the 1992–93 season.

losing to the Milwaukee Bucks in the Eastern Conference semi-finals. The Nets were ousted in the first round the next two years.

During the 1985–86 season, the Nets lost Richardson. He was thrown out of the NBA for breaking the league's rules against drugs. Richardson had tested positive for using cocaine.

Starting with 1986–87, the Nets missed the playoffs for five seasons in a row. The team did, however, win a lottery for the first pick in the 1990 NBA Draft. New Jersey selected forward Derrick Coleman from Syracuse University. Coleman scored 18.4 points per game in his first season and was the NBA Rookie of the Year.

With Coleman and long-range shooter Drazen Petrovic in the lineup, the Nets got back in the playoffs in 1991–92 despite having a 40–42 record. Coach Bill Fitch was fired after the season. Fitch had been second-guessed for not giving a lot of playing time to the Nets' number one draft pick, guard Kenny Anderson. That changed the next season. New coach Chuck Daly put Anderson in the starting lineup. The move was working fine until Anderson was injured in February and lost for the season. Still, New Jersey made the playoffs again.

After the season, the Nets were stunned by the death of Petrovic. In his final season, Petrovic averaged a team-best 22.3 points. Petrovic, who was from Croatia, was in Germany to visit his girlfriend when the car he was riding in collided with a tractor-trailer. He was 28 when he died. The Nets honored Petrovic by retiring his uniform No. 3 in 1993.

The Nets made the playoffs again in 1993–94 but were bounced in the first round by the rival New York Knicks. That began another series of unsuccessful seasons for New Jersey. From 1994–95 through 2000–01, the Nets made the playoffs just once, in 1997–98. That season, the Michael Jordan-led Chicago Bulls swept the Nets in the first round.

The Nets' next three seasons were a struggle as they barely won one-third of their games. Some players still performed well, though. Forward Keith Van Horn averaged about 20 points per game. So did guard Stephon Marbury. But the team would have to wait until 2001–02 to reach the heights of the NBA.

CHAPTER 6

NEW HOPE,
NEW BEGINNINGS

The Nets made a key change before the 2001–02 season by trading for Jason Kidd in a deal that included sending Stephon Marbury to the Phoenix Suns.

Kidd, like Marbury, was a point guard. Point guards are in charge of handling the ball most of the time and getting it to their teammates. Marbury compiled a good number of assists. But he had a reputation for taking too many shots himself. Kidd, on the other hand, was known for sharing the ball more and not shooting as much.

The 2001–02 Nets did share the ball. No one on the team averaged as many as 15 points. Three players—Kenyon Martin, Keith Van Horn, and Kidd—averaged from 14.7 to 14.9 points a game. Another, Kerry Kittles, averaged 13.4.

The Los Angeles Lakers swept the Nets in the NBA Finals in four games. But

The Nets' Jason Kidd gets ready to make a pass as the Toronto Raptors' Chris Childs looks on in February 2002. Kidd led the Nets to NBA Finals trips in 2002 and 2003.

The Nets' Kenyon Martin, *left*, battles the Spurs' Tim Duncan for control of the ball during the 2003 NBA Finals. San Antonio won in six games.

Giving His Best Effort

" *I gave everything I had. I tried to compete at the highest level, and I'll sleep good tonight because I left everything out there.*"
—*Jason Kidd, during the 2003 NBA Finals*

Kidd had a great postseason. In the Nets' 20 playoff games, his averages were 19.6 points, 9.1 assists, and 8.2 rebounds. Nets coach Byron Scott, who won three championships as a guard with the Lakers in the

1980s, praised Kidd's effort in the Finals: "Jason plays at 110 percent in every game. We need other guys to join him. That's the bottom line."

The next season, the Nets won 49 games. This was nearly as many victories as the season before. New Jersey went back to the NBA Finals. Kidd and Martin again had solid seasons. Richard Jefferson emerged as one of the team's top offensive options. He took up the slack for the traded Van Horn. Jefferson often made nightly sports highlights on television with his drives to the basket that ended in dunks.

Though the Nets lost in the Finals again, this time they won twice before falling to the San Antonio Spurs in six games. However, Martin, who had played like one of the NBA's top power forwards during the season, had trouble dealing with the Spurs' Tim Duncan. "I felt like I let my team down," Martin said.

Though they did not get back to the NBA Finals, the Nets continued to be a successful team. They made the playoffs the next four years. New Jersey finished first in its division twice and advanced to the second round of the playoffs three times. Kidd continued to lead the team. Twice he was even the Nets' top rebounder. This was quite an accomplishment for a guard. Guards do not often play close to the basket.

During the 2004–05 season, the Nets traded with the Toronto Raptors for guard Vince Carter. Carter was one of the NBA's most spectacular players. Before he came to the Nets, Carter thrilled fans in the Slam Dunk Contest held by the league at its All-Star Game. Carter averaged more than 20

Jay-Z

Rap star Jay-Z became part-owner of the Nets in 2004. He played a major role in helping the team move to his hometown of Brooklyn. Many believed having Jay-Z on board raised the team's profile. However, Jay-Z sold his piece of the ownership in April 2013 so he could work as a player agent. He said his job as an owner, but not a fan, was complete.

points a game for each of his four seasons with the Nets.

In 2007–08, New Jersey began to skid and ended up 34–48. Kidd was unhappy with the situation. The Nets traded him to the Dallas Mavericks during the season. After the season, they dealt Jefferson to the Milwaukee Bucks. For 2008–09, the Nets posted the same record, 34–48, and again missed the playoffs.

As disappointing as those two seasons were, the Nets were even worse in 2009–10. In fact, it appeared that they were on their way to becoming the worst NBA team of all time. The Nets avoided finishing with the league's poorest record ever. But not by much. They went 12–70. This was barely better than the 9–73 mark by the Philadelphia 76ers in 1972–73.

The Nets were not without talent, though. They had All-Star guard Devin Harris and a developing center, Brook Lopez. But all the losing took its toll. One newspaper report described home games this way: "The Izod Center has the atmosphere of a morgue."

The Nets were feeling hopeful for the future, however. In December 2009, the team was sold to Russian billionaire Mikhail Prokhorov. Then, in 2012, the team left for the Barclays Center in Brooklyn, New York. That finally put the Nets in New York City, right across the river from Manhattan.

The Brooklyn Nets added veterans Kevin Garnett, *left*, Paul Pierce, *center*, and Jason Terry, *right*, before the 2013–14 season.

The Nets had momentum when they arrived in Brooklyn. They had traded Harris and others for All-Star point guard Deron Williams midway through the 2010–11 season. Then they added sharpshooting guard Joe Johnson before moving to Brooklyn for the 2012–13 season. And Johnson teamed up with Williams and Lopez to lead the Nets back to the playoffs for the first time since 2007.

Still, Brooklyn lost in the first round. The team and its fans wanted to do better. So before the 2013–14 season, the Nets made some huge moves. They hired Kidd as coach. Then, in a blockbuster trade, they added forwards Kevin Garnett and Paul Pierce plus point guard Jason Terry. Nets fans hoped the aging stars could help bring the team its first NBA championship.

TIMELINE

1967 On October 23, the New Jersey Americans of the ABA play their first regular-season game ever. The Americans lose 110–107 to the Pittsburgh Pipers in Teaneck, New Jersey.

1970 The team, now called the New York Nets, signs high-scoring forward Rick Barry on September 2. The sharpshooting Barry would finish second in the ABA in scoring in both the 1970–71 and 1971–72 seasons.

1972 On May 20, the Nets lose 108–105 to the visiting Pacers as Indiana wins the ABA Finals four games to two.

1973 The Nets acquire forward Julius Erving on August 1 in a trade with the Virginia Squires. Erving would establish himself as perhaps the best player in history.

1974 The Nets defeat the visiting Utah Stars 111–100 on May 10 to win the ABA Finals four games to one and capture their first league championship.

1976 On May 13, the host Nets beat the Denver Nuggets 112–106 in Game 6 of the ABA Finals to claim a second league title.

1976 The Nets trade Erving to the Philadelphia 76ers on October 20.

1976 The Nets enter the NBA on June 17 along with Denver, the Indiana Pacers, and the San Antonio Spurs of the ABA.

1977 Beginning with the 1977–78 season, the team becomes known as the New Jersey Nets.

1981	On October 30, the Nets play their first game at the new Brendan Byrne Arena in East Rutherford, New Jersey. The New York Knicks beat the rival Nets 103–99.
1986	On February 25, the NBA bans Nets guard Micheal Ray Richardson from the league because of drug use.
1993	Nets standout guard Drazen Petrovic is killed in a car accident in Germany on June 7.
2002	With point guard Jason Kidd helping lead the way, the Nets finish the 2001–02 regular season with a 52–30 mark. New Jersey advances to its first NBA Finals but is swept in four games by the Los Angeles Lakers.
2003	The Nets—led by Kidd, fellow guard Kerry Kittles, and forwards Richard Jefferson and Kenyon Martin—return to the NBA Finals. New Jersey falls in six games to the Spurs.
2010	On April 12, the Nets play their last game at the East Rutherford, New Jersey, arena now called the Izod Center. The Nets lose 105–95 to the Charlotte Bobcats.
2011	The Nets acquire All-Star guard Deron Williams from the Utah Jazz in exchange for Devin Harris and others.
2012	The Brooklyn Nets play their first regular-season game in the Barclays Center, defeating the Toronto Raptors 107–100 on November 3.
2013	The Nets return to the playoffs for the first time since 2007 but lose in the first round. After the season, the team hires Jason Kidd as coach and adds forwards Kevin Garnett and Paul Pierce, and guard Jason Terry from the Boston Celtics.

QUICK STATS

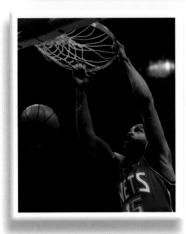

FRANCHISE HISTORY

New Jersey Americans (1967–68)
New York Nets (1968–77)
New Jersey Nets (1977–2012)
Brooklyn Nets (2012–)

NBA FINALS
(1978–)

2002, 2003

ABA FINALS
(1968–77; wins in bold)

1972, **1974**, **1976**

KEY PLAYERS
(position[s]; years with team)

Kenny Anderson (G; 1991–96)
Rick Barry (F; 1970–72)
Vince Carter (G/F; 2004–09)
Derrick Coleman (F; 1990–95)
Julius Erving (F/G; 1973–76)
Richard Jefferson (F; 2001–08)
Jason Kidd (G; 2001–08)
Bill Melchionni (G; 1969–76)
Billy Paultz (C/F; 1970–75)
Drazen Petrovic (G; 1991–93)
Buck Williams (F/C; 1981–89)
Deron Williams (G; 2011–)
John Williamson (G; 1973–77,
    1978–80)

KEY COACHES

Kevin Loughery (1973–80):
    297–318; 21–13 (postseason)
Byron Scott (2000–04):
    149–139; 25–15 (postseason)

HOME ARENAS

Teaneck Armory (1967–68)
Long Island Arena (1968–69)
Island Garden (1969–72)
Nassau Coliseum (1972–77)
Rutgers Athletic Center (1977–81)
Izod Center (1981–2010)
    Also known as Brendan Byrne
    Arena and Continental Airlines
    Arena
Prudential Center (2010–12)
Barclays Center (2012–)

* All statistics through 2012–13 season

QUOTES AND ANECDOTES

The Nets signed Lou Carnesecca, the coach of St. John's University in New York, to be their coach in 1969. But he could not join them until after his contract at St. John's was over. So York Larese had to coach the team for one season before Carnesecca joined the Nets in 1970.

"I love the game. I love to play. I'd play for nothing if everybody else did. But when in Rome, live as the Romans do." —Former Nets star forward Julius Erving, on enjoying basketball

Julius Erving's most famous dunk came during a contest, the first of its kind in professional basketball, at halftime of the 1976 ABA All-Star Game in Denver. Erving took off from the foul line and slammed it home, helping him outduel David Thompson of the Nuggets.

"When you play a game in any sport, you have a 50–50 chance of winning. But when you get involved in the drug game, there's a 100 percent chance you're going to lose." —Former Nets guard Micheal Ray Richardson, on his drug problems

Forward Chris Morris, who was with the Nets from 1988 to 1995, once showed how much he wanted to leave the team by writing "Trade me" on the sneakers that he wore during a game.

"You couldn't have wanted a better teammate. He was very talented, he played very hard and was able to lead by his example. He was indefatigable." —Former Nets coach Chuck Daly, on guard Drazen Petrovic

GLOSSARY

acquire

To add a player, usually through the draft, free agency, or a trade.

armory

A building used to store weapons or military equipment.

assist

A pass that leads directly to a made basket.

broadcaster

An announcer who describes or talks about sporting events on television or radio.

charter member

Someone who is there at the beginning.

compile

To put together.

franchise

An entire sports organization, including the players, coaches, and staff.

general manager

The executive who is in charge of the team's overall operation. He or she hires and fires managers and coaches, drafts players, and signs free agents.

interim

Temporary.

playoffs

A series of games in which the winners advance in a quest to win a championship.

rebound

To secure the basketball after a missed shot.

roster

The players as a whole on a basketball team.

trade

A move in which a player or players are sent from one team to another.

FOR MORE INFORMATION

Further Reading

Ballard, Chris. *The Art of a Beautiful Game: The Thinking Fan's Tour of the NBA*. New York: Simon & Schuster, 2009.

Mallozzi, Vincent, with Dave Anderson. *Doc: The Rise and Rise of Julius Erving*. Hoboken, NJ: Wiley & Sons, 2009.

Simmons, Bill. *The Book of Basketball: The NBA According to the Sports Guy*. New York: Random House, 2009.

Web Links

To learn more about the Brooklyn Nets, visit ABDO Publishing Company online at **www.abdopublishing.com**. Web sites about the Nets are featured on our Book Links page. These links are routinely monitored and updated to provide the most current information available.

Places to Visit

Barclays Center
620 Atlantic Avenue
Brooklyn, NY 11217
917-618-6700
www.barclayscenter.com
This has been the Nets' home arena since their move to Brooklyn in 2012. The team plays 41 regular-season games here each season.

Naismith Memorial Basketball Hall of Fame
1000 West Columbus Avenue
Springfield, MA 01105
413-781-6500
www.hoophall.com
This hall of fame and museum highlights the greatest players and moments in the history of basketball. Julius Erving and Rick Barry are among the former Nets enshrined here.

Nassau Veterans Memorial Coliseum
1255 Hempstead Turnpike
Long Island, NY 11553
516-794-9300
www.nassaucoliseum.com
Home of the New York Islanders of the National Hockey League, this arena was where the Nets played when they won two ABA championships.

INDEX

About the Author

Ray Frager is a freelance writer based in the Baltimore, Maryland, area. He has been a professional sports editor and writer since 1980. He has worked for the *Trenton Times*, the *Dallas Morning News*, the *Baltimore Sun*, and FOXSports.com. At the *Baltimore Sun*, he edited books on Cal Ripken Jr., the building of Baltimore's football stadium, and the Baltimore Ravens' 2000 Super Bowl season. He has written books on the Baltimore Orioles and the Pittsburgh Pirates.